PALLET CRAFT

2

PALLET CRAFT

20 CREATIVE MAKES USING WOODEN PALLETS

Emma Basden

First published 2018 by
Guild of Master Craftsman Publications Ltd
Castle Place, 166 High Street, Lewes,
East Sussex BN7 1XU

ISBN 978 1 78494 486 5

PUBLISHER
Jonathan Bailey

PRODUCTION
Jim Bulley & Jo Pallett

SENIOR PROJECT EDITOR
Dominique Page

EDITOR
Nicola Hodgson

MANAGING ART EDITOR
Gilda Pacitti

DESIGN & ART DIRECTION
Wayne Blades

PHOTOGRAPHY
Neal Grundy and Emma Basden

PICTURE CREDITS
Tool icons on pp. 8, 10, 13, 14 and cover:
Shutterstock/vvushakovv

Colour origination by GMC Reprographics
Printed and bound in China

CONTENTS

Creating interesting, useful and beautiful things out of wood has always been a huge passion of mine. I inherited it from my father, who taught me so much when I was a child. We turned doors into unusual tables, made shelves out of old floorboards and decorated our various homes together.

This book combines my passion for working with wood and the growing trend for recycling and upcycling pieces of interest for people's homes. Instead of buying new items, I enjoy the challenge of refurbishing something old, or the process of transforming basic materials into something special. It is also a great way to participate in saving the planet.

Pallets play beautifully into this trend, as they are accessible, affordable and attractive. You don't need to be a highly experienced woodworker or have a lot of specialist tools to make something out of a pallet. I have been using pallets to add detail to my home for years now, and within the pages of this book I will show you how to create a few of my favourite designs. I hope you enjoy making them!

Emma Basden

LEFT
Pallets offer a cheap and fun way to create unique furniture and home accessories.

OPPOSITE
A great addition to the garden or playroom, children will love to hide out in a tipi (see page 110).

SOURCING PALLETS

The key to making an attractive and well-finished project out of recycled pallets is to use clean ones that are in good condition. Here are some tips for sourcing them affordably or – better still – for free.

If you look carefully, you'll be surprised at how often you spot discarded pallets in skips or at recycling centres. However, there are lots of businesses that are worth asking if they have unwanted pallets you can take away. Building sites are a great starting point because most building materials are delivered on pallets. You'll find that a lot of builders are more than happy to let you take away the ones you want.

Garden centres, bathroom and furniture stores are other useful places to check out, as they can get inundated with pallets. Always ask before you take one, though, as larger companies sometimes have a system in place to get refunds on returned pallets.

Smaller businesses are also well worth a look: they often have a weekly delivery of stock and end up with a pile of pallets at the back of their store. The smaller companies are left to dispose of their pallets, so you may be doing them a favour by taking a few. Try making friends with the owners and show them the projects you are making. If they feel involved in what you are doing, they may be happy to keep you in stock.

If you are looking for several pallets to make a larger project, you might want to visit a local pallet supplier and persuade them to let you look around their yard. They may have slightly damaged ones that they will let you take for free, but you can buy pallets in great condition for very little. If you buy several pallets and live locally, they may deliver for a small fee.

Lastly, don't underestimate the power of the Internet. Searching local community pages can be a great way to source pallets. More often than not, these pallets are free if you are able to collect them.

Different types of pallets

There are three different types of pallets available:

American pallets are usually made from hardwood, which fares better outdoors. They also come with a nice curve in the supports, which lends detail to projects. The typical dimensions of an American pallet are 48 x 40in (122 x 102cm).

European pallets come in two varieties: one with hardwood blocks that hold them together, and one with chipwood blocks. The latter are best for indoor projects, as chipwood will eventually disintegrate in the rain. The typical dimensions of a European pallet are 31½ x 47¼in (80 x 120cm).

International pallets are larger than standard-sized European and American pallets, and are used for shipping. Pallet suppliers break down and sell the planks from them, which can be up to 13ft (4m) in length. These are ideal if you need lengths of wood that are longer than a standard pallet.

OPPOSITE
Pallets are available to source from many businesses, including designated pallet suppliers.

DISMANTLING PALLETS

Before starting a pallet project, you need to dismantle it without breaking or damaging any of the boards. Most wood stores will dismantle pallets and sell the planks for a very reasonable cost. This is convenient and cost-effective. However, if you have found some discarded pallets, or simply want to try dismantling them yourself, there are several possible methods.

NOTE: Dismantling a pallet can be dangerous, so ensure you wear appropriate safety gear. You will need heavy-duty work gloves as protection from splinters, and safety goggles to avoid bits of wood or old nails getting into your eyes.

1. Hammer
2. Hammer and brick chisel
3, 4 & 5. Hammer and crowbar
6. Reciprocating saw

Using a hammer

This method can only be used on the European style of pallet (see page 10). Start off by hitting the blocks that hold the two sides of the pallet together to loosen them. Then continue to tap the planks in a downwards direction until they separate from the blocks. This is time-consuming but effective.

Using a hammer and brick chisel

Place the chisel between the board and the support to which it is attached. Hit the chisel with the hammer so that the chisel breaks the nail. Continue this until all of the planks are released.

Using a hammer and crowbar

Place the crowbar between the board and the support and tap it with the hammer until it is secure beneath the board. Pry the board using the crowbar as a lever, then tap the boards as they come up to release them.

Using a reciprocating saw

Use a reciprocating saw to cut through the nails sideways so that the board is released from the supports intact. This is the easiest way to dismantle a pallet with minimal damage.

BASIC KIT

Having the right tools and materials to hand before you start a project is half the battle won. Here are the basic items required, but always check the tools and materials lists before you start to make sure you have everything you need.

Handsaw

A good handsaw will save you time and energy. For pallet builds, you will need a general-purpose saw, normally called a panel saw. This is the general 'go-to' saw for any DIY enthusiast.

Jigsaw

A jigsaw with sharp blades can cut both straight and curved lines, helping you to tackle tricky corners. They are available corded or cordless; I prefer the freedom of movement afforded by a cordless one. There is a range of blades for different purposes, so make sure you get the right blades for the job.

Reciprocating saw/hammer and brick chisel/hammer and crowbar

You can use a hammer and brick chisel or crowbar to dismantle pallets (see pages 12–13), but the easiest option is to use a reciprocating saw. You don't need a top-of-the range one, although the better the saw the faster it will do the job. It works by using a push/pull cutting action and has settings that allow you to change the speed depending on what you are cutting: faster speeds for soft materials such as wood, and slower ones for harder materials such as metal.

Sander

A power sander can complete a job in minutes that might take hours by hand. There are many models available, but I recommended a palm sander: they are reasonably priced, lightweight, can be operated with one hand, and can complete most of the jobs you ask of it. If your projects feature tight corners, consider buying an electric detail sander. This has a triangular base plate that allows you to get right into the corners.

Sandpaper

Sandpaper is graded based upon the number of abrasive particles per square inch. Therefore, the lower the number, the coarser the grit: coarse (40–60 grit); medium (80–120); fine (150–180); very fine (220–240); extra-fine (280–320) and super-fine (360 and above). If you have a pallet that is quite rough and dirty, you might need to start with a low-grit coarse paper to take the dirt off, then finish with a high-grit medium-to-fine paper to smooth it off. 120-grit is a good all-rounder for pallet projects.

Drill

Your drill will be your best friend when embarking on a pallet project. There are many drills on the market and decent ones are available at a reasonable price. Cordless drills are useful as they give you more freedom to move around. Keep the spare battery charged; there is nothing worse than it dying on you halfway through a project!

Drill bits

Make sure you have the correct drill bits handy before starting a project. Wood drill bits for making pilot holes can ensure that your screws go in smoothly without splitting the wood. Before you buy everything separately, see if you can make a saving by buying a box set with everything you need to start you off.

Flat bit or spade bit

A flat bit or spade bit is used in your drill to make different-sized holes. Each bit has the dimension of the hole that it cuts marked on it. Place the point in the centre of where you want the hole cut, hold it straight, and let the drill do the rest.

Wood screws

There are many different types and sizes of wood screws; green ones are a good choice as they stand out less than silver or gold ones. You can build most projects in this book using $1^1/_4$in (30mm) and $1^1/_2$in (40mm) wood screws, which are available in any hardware store.

Tape measure or ruler

Measure twice, cut once! This invaluable tip has helped me throughout my DIY career. Your tape measure will allow you to measure correctly to any length, short or long, and ensure that you get all your planks cut to the right size. Make your cutting marks with a pencil or marker pen.

Square and combination square

A square is useful when you need to mark a perfect 90-degree angle before you cut. The combination square has various uses, including marking out a square with specific dimensions, or measuring and marking a perfect 45-degree angle – this is especially useful when creating a frame where the edges need to meet up exactly.

Chalk paint

Chalk paint is a great way to add some colour to your projects without obscuring the beauty of the wood grain. Give your planks a good coat of chalk paint, let it dry, then sand back the paint so you are left with a light, chalky covering of colour to achieve a 'shabby chic' look.

Paintbrush

Another useful saying is: buy cheap, buy twice. All DIY shops have a good selection of paintbrushes; make sure you buy a good-quality brush that you can use time and time again.

Beeswax

For a natural finish to your project, take a clean cloth, apply a good amount of beeswax, then rub it into the wood. This gives the wood a smooth, silky finish and enhances the beauty of the grain.

Wood stain

Wood stains are available in many different colours, and also in indoor and outdoor finishes, so make sure you choose the right one for your purpose. To apply wood stain, use a clean paintbrush and simply brush it on.

1. Safety goggles
2. Handsaw
3. Combination square
4. Hammer and crowbar
5. Flat bit
6. Good-quality paintbrush
7. Set square

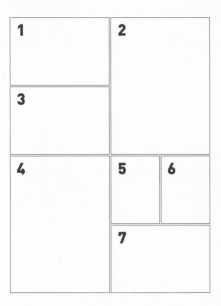

Wood filler

Wood filler is handy if you want to fill in the gaps between planks in projects such as the Headboard (see page 124) or Coffee Table (see page 90), or to cover over screw heads once you have countersunk them, as in the Home Bar project (see page 78). Buy a natural wood colour, apply it, wipe off any excess filler, wait for it to dry, then sand it down.

Wood glue

Wood glue bonds to wood. It comes in different strengths, so choose the right one for the job. Most wood glues need clamping so the wood doesn't move, giving the glue the best chance of setting. With some of the projects in this book, screwing the pieces together will suffice, but if you want to give a piece extra strength, adding wood glue is a good idea.

Safety goggles and gloves

Your safety is paramount. Wear safety glasses or goggles to protect your eyes when sanding, cutting or drilling and heavy-duty work gloves to protect from splinters.

GARDEN
ARMCHAIR
page 40

WINE CADDY
page 46

COAT &
BOOT RACK
page 50

DOG BED
page 56

VINTAGE STAR
page 62

FESTIVE TREE
page 66

BOOK RACK
page 70

LEAN-TO
SHELVING
page 74

HOME BAR
page 78

SWING SEAT
page 84

COFFEE TABLE
page 90

TOWEL RAIL
SHELVES
page 96

FOOTSTOOL
page 100

WINE RACK
page 106

TIPI
page 110

DARTBOARD
HOUSING
page 116

SIDE TABLE

page 120

HEADBOARD

page 124

GARDEN BENCH
page 130

BATH RACK

page 136

THE
PROJECTS

GARDEN ARMCHAIR

This outdoor tub chair is very comfortable. It is the perfect shape and height to nestle in, rest a drink on its arm, and relax in the sun. To make a seat cushion that fits perfectly, you will need to measure the seat space and cut a piece of foam to size. If you are not handy with a sewing machine, then why not ask a friend who sews if they can make you a cover?

YOU WILL NEED

2 x standard-sized pallets (American pallets were used here for their shaped detailing) plus approx. 33–39ft (10–12m) pallet planks

Handsaw or jigsaw

Tape measure or ruler

Pencil or marker pen

Drill

Wood drill bit

1¼in (30mm) and 4in (100mm) wood screws

Sander and sandpaper (120-grit)

1 x cushion for the seat

1 x cushion for the back

So cool - So fragrant

STEP ONE

Take one of the pallets and place it the right way up on the ground. Cut it down the middle lengthways, cutting to one side of the central support so that it's left intact on one side, as shown in the photograph opposite.

STEP TWO

Take the half of the pallet that still has the central support attached to it; put the other half aside. Place the half-pallet upside down on the ground and remove the middle plank. Now turn it over and remove the middle plank from the other side.

STEP THREE

Measure the half-pallet lengthways and mark the centre point on the two supports either side. Cut the pallet in half again, leaving you with two parts.

STEP FOUR

Take one of the halves, turn it upside down and lay it on the ground. Each side of the pallet's supports has a semicircle shape cut out. You need to square off one end of the curve (on both sides): this is where the seat will be attached later. Make sure you square off the right end: it should be the one nearest the foot of the side, not the top.

STEP FIVE

Make your cuts. Repeat this process on the other half of the pallet. These sections will form the two sides of the armchair.

STEP SIX

To make the seat for the armchair, take the other pallet and cut it in half lengthways. Again using the side that has both the side and middle supports still attached, decide how wide you want your armchair to be. Cut the pallet in half widthways to your chosen measurement. Stand the two sides up opposite each other and place the seat between them, resting the seat onto the four right angles you cut earlier. Attach the seat into place with 4in (100mm) wood screws. Use a wood drill bit to make a pilot hole first, and the screw will go much more easily.

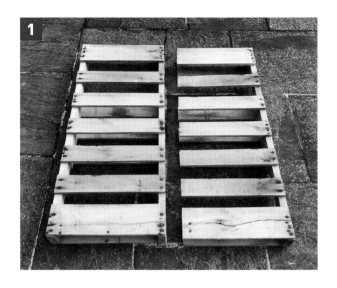

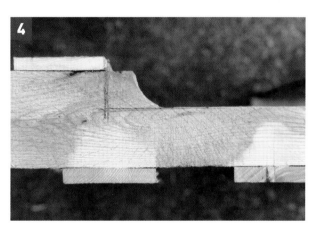

STEP SEVEN

With the sides and seat now attached, turn the chair onto its front so that you can work on the back. Measure the width of the back and cut lengths of pallet planks to fit across. Screw them in with your 1¼in (30mm) wood screws, all the way down to the bottom of the chair as far as you can go. The final plank will need to be cut to the exact width, as it might not reach the very bottom or might stick out below the feet; go as far as you can, as it is possible to add the final layer of planks later on.

STEP EIGHT

For the sides, there will already be a few planks in place, but to make the sides solid you will need to attach planks to fill the gaps. Measure the gaps, then cut the planks to the right width and length and attach with 1¼in (30mm) wood screws.

STEP NINE

Repeat this on both sides, then fill the gaps in the seat with planks again.

STEP TEN

Measure the front of the chair's width and cut and attach planks underneath the seat part. Measure and cut the final planks for the back and sides to finish off the chair. Bring the planks down to the bottom of the chair and attach with 1¼in (30mm) wood screws. To finish off the back and sides of the chair, attach two planks to the top of the arms, and cut and attach a ⅝in (15mm)-wide length of plank along the back of the chair.

STEP ELEVEN

Sand the chair all over. Place a large cushion on the seat and a smaller one behind it to create a comfortable back for the chair.

WINE CADDY

Be the envy of any picnic or summer party when you arrive bearing a bottle of wine and two glasses in this stylish caddy! If you are feeling up to the challenge, you could adjust the design so that it holds four glasses.

YOU WILL NEED

1 x pallet plank (any type)

1 x wine bottle

2 x wine glasses

Tape measure or ruler

Pencil or marker pen

Jigsaw

Sander and sandpaper (120-grit)

Drill

1½in (40mm) wood screws

Flat bit (approx. ⅝–¾in/16–20mm, to create a hole big enough to fit the rope through)

Rope to use as handle – approx. 12–18in (30–45cm) length (suggested thickness: ⅝–¾in/16–20mm)

STEP ONE

Take a pallet plank and place your two wine glasses and wine bottle in position, ensuring there is enough space between them for your partition wood. Measure how long the bottom of your caddy will need to be, draw a line and cut the plank. Sand each piece as you go, as it will be hard to sand once it is completed.

STEP TWO

Cut two more pieces of plank to the same length as the bottom of the caddy. These pieces will make the sides later on. Put them aside for now.

STEP THREE

Cut two pieces of plank to approximately 6¾in (17cm). These will form the ends of the caddy.

STEP FOUR

Take the two ends you have just cut and place them on their ends. Attach the bottom of the caddy to these with the 1½in (40mm) wood screws.

STEP FIVE

To create the two centre supports (to which you will attach the rope handle at the very end), cut two pieces of plank to approximately 16in (40cm) long. Use the jigsaw to cut out an arch at one end of each plank to give the planks a rounded 'nose'.

STEP SIX

Next you will need your flat bit to make a hole so that you can attach the rope to create the handle.

STEP SEVEN

Attach both of the planks to the bottom of the caddy in the same way as you attached the ends. Stand your wine glasses and bottle in the caddy to work out the best place to position the two middle supports before you attach them.

STEP EIGHT

Take the two sides you cut earlier and attach them to the caddy. You should have two even holes in the middle supports. Take the rope and thread it through these holes, tying knots in both ends to create a sturdy handle for carrying.

COAT & BOOT RACK

This coat and boot rack will add style to any hallway: no more hanging coats on the backs of doors! It incorporates a shoe tidy and a bench seat for a space-saving multi-purpose item. Paint it white for a Scandinavian-inspired look, or leave the boards bare for a 'shabby chic' finish.

YOU WILL NEED

International pallet planks for the back, plus standard-sized planks for the rest (the number required depends on the size of rack you want to make)

Tape measure or ruler

Pencil

Handsaw

White chalk paint and paintbrush (optional)

1½in (40mm) wood screws

Drill

Jigsaw

Sander and sandpaper (120-grit)

Coat hooks and small screws

STEP ONE

First, decide how tall and how wide you want your coat and boot rack to be. These dimensions will serve as a guide to how wide or tall you need to cut your planks. Starting with the back of the rack, cut your long planks to the height you want. Use as many as you need to create the width. Once they are cut to size, lay them on your workbench or on a flat surface side by side so that they are equally lined up. Measure the full width of them put together. Cut two pieces of wood to that length to serve as batons that will hold the back together. One will be slightly shorter at the bottom (the thickness of one plank either side) as this will allow the seat/boot rack to slot perfectly against the back either side of it. The third plank (under the first, shown in the photo opposite) is where you will attach the coat hooks: make sure it is high enough to allow a coat to be hung up. I also painted my two planks with white chalk paint. I cut my boards to 75in (190cm) and used seven boards to create a width of 27½in (70cm).

STEP TWO

Cut six planks to the height you want your seat to be. These planks will form the sides of your seat. I cut mine to 20in (50cm). Put three planks together and cut another plank to the size of the width of the three put together. Attach the wood with 1½in (40mm) wood screws to all three planks and cut another to attach to the top. Repeat this process with the other three planks to create the second side.

STEP THREE

Cut six more planks to the width of the back of the rack. These will form the top of the seat. Stand the seat sides on their ends and place three of the planks on top. Use two screws in each plank to ensure they are fixed firmly in place.

STEP FOUR

Place the remaining three planks on top of those you have just attached to create a thicker and sturdier seat. Fix them with screws to the planks beneath.

STEP FIVE

Now make the boot rack. Stand your seat up and measure the gap between the two sides. Cut three planks to this size and position them as shown. Secure them with screws, then sand the boot rack and seat.

STEP SIX

Stand the back of the rack up and put the boot rack/seat in position. It should fit perfectly up against the back, with the bottom support you attached to the back earlier fitting perfectly inbetween the sides and underneath the boot shelf. This will allow you to attach the seat/boot rack and the back together using 1½in (40mm) wood screws.

STEP SEVEN

Position the back piece behind the rack/seat. Fix the two parts together using screws inserted in the rear of the stand. Ensure each plank is attached with a screw to pull the two parts tight together.

STEP EIGHT

Cut a plank to attach to the top of the back, making it a little longer than the width of the back. This will finish off the rack neatly; it can also serve as a shelf for extra storage.

STEP NINE

The final touch is to add the coat hooks. I sourced mine from my local wood shop, but they are readily available online or from any hardware store.

DOG BED

This dog bed design is simple, looks great and is a tasteful replacement for the chewed-up cushion or basket that many dogs sleep in. If you paint or stain this item, make sure the product you use is animal-friendly, particularly as so many dogs love to chew.

YOU WILL NEED

Planks from 2 pallets (any type; the number required depends on the size of dog bed you want to make)
1 x 1in (25 x 25mm) wooden batten (for corner supports)
Tape measure or ruler
Pencil or marker pen
Handsaw or jigsaw
Sander and sandpaper (120-grit)
Drill
¾in (20mm) and 1½in (40mm) wood screws
Animal-friendly stain (optional)
Paintbrush (optional)

NOTE:
It is essential that every plank you use is sanded down properly and any corners rounded off to ensure the dog's safety.

STEP ONE

Decide where you are going to put the bed and make sure the dimensions of your bed don't exceed the space. This bed is 31½ x 19¾in (80 x 50cm). Cut six planks to 19¾in (50cm) in length. Sand them down well (see note on page 56) and put three aside. Lay the first three next to each other and measure the width across to determine what size to cut your batten to; these batten pieces will serve as the supports. Cut the batten to the desired length, place a piece at the top and bottom of the three planks, and secure with 1½in (40mm) wood screws. Repeat this process with the second three planks. These will form the two sides of the dog bed. Put these aside for a moment.

STEP TWO

Prepare the back and front of the bed. Cut three more planks 31½in (80cm) in length (the width of the bed) to create the back, then one more piece to 31½in (80cm); this will serve as the bottom plank at the front of the bed.

STEP THREE

To create the opening at the front, cut four pieces of shorter plank and cut a diagonal line down to the bottom plank. These planks can be sanded now or when you finish.

STEP FOUR

Cut these to shape, then turn them over and lay them onto the two planks the other side to ensure the angle is exactly the same.

STEP FIVE

Draw a line and remove the unwanted part. Cut the other two planks along the same lines. You should have four pieces of plank that create a symmetrical opening to the bed.

STEP SIX

Go back to the two sides made in step one. Find an even floor space to stand these up on their ends. Take the three planks you cut earlier to form the back of the bed. Lay them across the top of the ends and secure to the battens attached to the sides with the 1½in (40mm) wood screws. The three sides of the bed are now attached together securely.

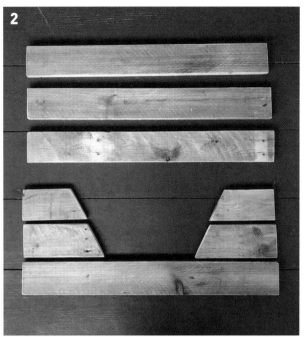

STEP SEVEN

Because the front has been cut into a V-shape, we need to strengthen it before attaching it to the sides. Lay down the pieces that form the front and make sure they are lined up evenly. Lay them so that the backs of the boards are facing upwards; when you secure the front to the bed, the framework will lie hidden on the inside. Take a new plank and cut it horizontally down the middle. You will use these pieces to create a frame on the inside of the front to hold the planks securely together. Cut the pieces as shown opposite and secure them using ¾in (20mm) wood screws. Cut the top piece of batten so it sits 1in (25mm) or so away from the edge, so that the front can be fitted in snugly against the batten to which it will be secured.

STEP EIGHT

Attach the front of the bed in the same way you did for the back using 1½in (40mm) wood screws.

STEP NINE

Turn the bed upside down to expose the bottom. Cut your lengths of plank to size to attach to the bottom using the 1½in (40mm) wood screws. Lastly, if you want to stain or paint the bed, do so now, making sure that you use animal-friendly materials.

VINTAGE STAR

This star makes a striking focal point for any room. Hang it above a bed or a fireplace, lean it against a wall, or wrap it up and give it to someone special. A coat of chalk paint will give it a vintage look, but bare boards also look effective.

YOU WILL NEED

Pallet planks (any type; size and number required
    depend on the size of star you want to make)
Handsaw or jigsaw
Chalk paint and paintbrush (optional)
Sander and sandpaper (120-grit)
Drill
1¼in (30mm) wood screws
String
Pencil
Pin
Straight edge or ruler

STEP ONE

Cut the pallet planks to the length required so you can draw on your desired size of five-point star. To create a vintage look, as used here, paint some of the planks with chalk paint, then lightly sand them to achieve a distressed effect.

STEP TWO

Lay the planks side by side, face down, to create a square. Lay an extra plank horizontally across them and drill a few screws into it to temporarily hold the planks together while you draw a star on the other side.

STEP THREE

To draw a neat star, first draw a circle the size you want the star to be. To do this, take a length of string (the length will be the radius of the circle), a pencil and a pin. Anchor one end of the string to the centre of the planks with the pin. Tie the pencil to the other end of the string. Draw a circle while pulling the pencil tight on the string. If the string is kept taut, you should draw a perfect circle. Now, using a pencil and a ruler, draw an upside-down V inside the circle, with each point touching the edges of the circle. Next, draw a line from the bottom right point across to the middle far left edge of the circle. Draw straight across to the opposite side, then down across to the left to meet your first point. You should have a nice, neat star.

STEP FOUR

Once you are happy with the size and look of the star, remove the support plank from the back of the planks. Lay each piece on a flat surface to be cut using a jigsaw or handsaw.

STEP FIVE

Once all the planks have been cut, place them back into position and check the star still looks good. Sand off any rough edges.

STEP SIX

Turn the pieces over to reveal the back of the star. Cut small pieces of plank into the shapes necessary to hold the star together and drill these pieces in place. You can now turn the star around and admire the finished result!

FESTIVE TREE

Rather than chopping down a fir tree to use for a single season, why not make a sustainable pallet tree that you can use time and again? Adorn it with lights, hang baubles from it or keep it simple and plain. Whichever way, this tree adds a touch of Nordic style to the festive season.

YOU WILL NEED

1 x pallet (any type)
Ruler or tape measure
Pencil
Handsaw or jigsaw
Hammer
Sander and sandpaper (120-grit)
Drill
1¼in (30mm) wood screws
Fairy lights (optional)

STEP ONE

Take a pallet and lay it down on an even surface. Take a ruler and a pencil and mark the top of your tree in the middle of the support post that will hold your tree together (acting as the trunk of the tree). Mark two points at the bottom of the pallet to the far left and right. Draw your two cut lines from the centre point outwards to the two points, giving you a triangular tree shape.

STEP TWO

With a jigsaw or handsaw, cut along the lines through the pallet slats. If there are any slats attached to the rear of the support post, knock them off with a hammer.

STEP THREE

You should now have a tree shape. Remove the bottom plank to create the base of the tree. You will attach the stand to this in the next step. Sand the tree down so that all the edges are smooth.

STEP FOUR

Cut two pieces of the excess planks to around 12in (30cm) in length, sand them down and, using your drill and 1¼in (30mm) wood screws, attach them either side of the bottom of the tree to the support post. Your tree should now stand up.

STEP FIVE

The final step, if you choose to do so, is to dress the tree with fairy lights. I used copper wire fairy lights here, as the wire is discreet and keeps the tree looking clean and simple.

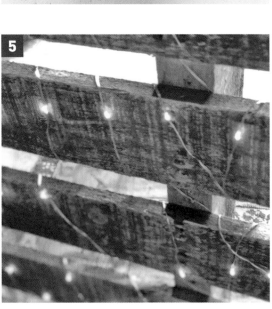

BOOK RACK

Having extra storage space is a positive asset in most people's houses, and this stylish wooden book rack will provide just that, while adding handmade rustic charm to any room. This is a relatively simple project to make; you'll find most of the hard work is in the sanding and finishing.

YOU WILL NEED

1 x pallet (any type; an American pallet was used here for its shaped detailing)
Tape measure or ruler
Pencil
Handsaw
Sander and sandpaper (120-grit)
Drill
1½in (40mm) wood screws
Wood stain and a cloth to apply it

STEP ONE

Take a pallet and turn it upside down on a flat surface. Using a pencil, mark cutting guidelines on all three supports that run through the pallet at either end of the second plank from the bottom.

STEP TWO

Using a handsaw, cut along the three supports attached to the plank that will form the top of your book rack. You should be left with a portion of the pallet that looks like the photograph opposite.

STEP THREE

Take your sander and smooth off any rough edges, taking time to smooth the three curves at the end of the supports. This will give your shelf a professional finish.

STEP FOUR

Next, cut a length of plank to fit the bottom of the book rack and attach it to the supports' ends and middle with the 1¹⁄₂in (40mm) wood screws.

STEP FIVE

This particular pallet was quite light in colour. You can use a wood stain, applied with a cloth, to impart a more vintage-style look to the wood, as I did here. Leave the stain to dry, then lightly sand the book rack again to mellow the stain.

LEAN-TO SHELVING

This leaning shelf unit not only looks great but is also perfect for displaying your favourite books, photo frames or ceramics without taking up too much space in the living room or bedroom. It would also be ideal storage for toiletries and perfume bottles in the bathroom.

YOU WILL NEED

3 x international pallet planks for base
4 x standard-sized pallet planks for shelves and brackets
Tape measure or ruler
Pencil
Handsaw or jigsaw
Sander and sandpaper (120-grit)
Drill
1¼in (30mm) wood screws
Square or right-angle ruler

STEP ONE

Take three international pallet planks and cut them to approximately 67in (170cm) in length. Sand them well and lay them on a flat surface or workbench.

STEP TWO

Measure the width of the planks when pushed up tightly together. In this case, the width was 12in (30cm). Cut two pieces of standard-sized plank to this width.

STEP THREE

Attach these two pieces of plank to the rear of the other planks, top and bottom, to secure the planks together.

STEP FOUR

Next, cut six more pieces of plank to 12in (30cm): three will form the brackets and three will form the shelves. Sand all the pieces thoroughly, rounding off any sharp edges or corners. Take the three pieces for the brackets and lay them where you want the shelves to be. Using a square or right-angle ruler, make sure they are straight, then attach them with 1¼in (30mm) wood screws.

STEP FIVE

Once the brackets are in place, put the pieces that will form the shelves at a right angle up against the top of the brackets. Attach the shelves to the bracket with 1¼in (30mm) wood screws.

STEP SIX

Stand the shelving unit up and make sure that the shelves are straight and at perfect right angles. Make any necessary adjustments.

HOME BAR

If you enjoy entertaining at home, this bar – which will work indoors or outside – will be the focal point of all your parties. Paint it to harmonize with your interior décor, or keep it natural for a rustic addition to a garden.

YOU WILL NEED

2 x pallets (any type, but if it's to be used outside then it's best if they're hardwood), plus plenty of extra planks

1 x length of wooden joist approximately 12 x 56in (30 x 140cm)

Tools to remove planks (see page 14)

Handsaw or jigsaw

Drill

1¼in (30mm), 1½in (40mm) and 4in (100mm) wood screws

Sander and sandpaper (120-grit)

Drill bit

Countersink drill bit

Tape measure or ruler

Wood filler

STEP ONE

Take a pallet and cut it in half widthways. Lay the two halves of the pallet on the ground and remove all the planks (see page 13) except for the ones at the ends. You don't want any gaps in the bar, so you need to place the slats back down, but next to one another.

STEP TWO

You will need extra slats, so have some already removed from another pallet, or buy ready-bought pallet planks cut to size. Lay the pallet slats back down onto the frame next to each other and secure them with 4in (100mm) wood screws. Repeat this process on the other half. These will form the sides of the bar.

STEP THREE

For the front of the bar, take another pallet and, keeping this one whole, repeat the same process used to create the sides: remove all of the slats, then re-lay them, placing in additional ones to ensure the entire pallet front is covered.

STEP FOUR

Stand all three sides up and put them together to create the bar shape.

STEP FIVE

Once you are happy with the way it fits together, using 4in (100mm) wood screws, attach the two sides to the front, going in with the screws from the sides into the front. This will hold all three sides in place.

STEP SIX

When you look at the bar from the front, you will see two gaps either side of the front section where the front and sides meet. Using another pallet plank, attach this to the gaps either side to finish off the bar front using 1½in (40mm) wood screws.

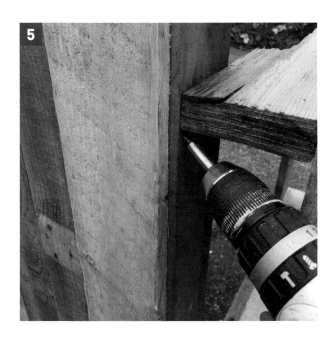

STEP SEVEN

Go behind the bar to measure the space between the two sides and cut a plank to that size. This will act as the shelf for glasses. Using two small sections of pallet plank as brackets for the shelf, screw the brackets to the sides using 1¼in (30mm) wood screws, lay the shelf onto them and screw the plank to the brackets. This will also strengthen the bar by attaching the sides to each other.

STEP EIGHT

For the top of your bar, you could simply use lengths of pallet planks. However, to give the bar a more solid top, a length of wooden joist was used for this project. Joists are easy to find in any wood store and are very cheap. Cut one length of the joist to the length of the bar and then cut two shorter pieces for the sides.

STEP NINE

Attach the top sections of the bar using wood screws. The length of the screws required will depend on the thickness of the top that you choose; for this project, 4in (100mm) screws were used. Make pilot holes with a drill bit prior to attaching them.

STEP TEN

To sink the screws, use a countersink drill bit that creates a dip for the screw head to go deeper into the wood. Once secure and in place, use wood filler to cover the screw heads.

SWING SEAT

If you have a tree that is sturdy enough to take the weight of a swing, then this project will really add something to your garden. Big enough for two, there will be no need to argue over whose turn it is next.

YOU WILL NEED

1 x standard-sized pallet (an American pallet was used here for its shaped detailing and durability outside), plus extra pallet planks

Paint and paintbrush

Sander and sandpaper (120-grit)

Drill

1¼in (30mm) and 1½in (40mm) wood screws

Beeswax and clean cloth to apply it

Flat bit (approx. ¼in/20mm, or big enough to fit the rope through)

Tape measure or ruler

Jigsaw

Heavy-duty scissors

Rope to suspend swing – approx. 33ft (10m) length (suggested thickness: ⅝–¾in/ 15–20mm in nylon or hemp)

STEP ONE

Take a pallet and place it the right way up on the ground. Cut the pallet in half lengthways, cutting to one side of the central support.

STEP TWO

Cut lengths of planks to fit into the gaps between the pallet slats. You might have to make some of them thinner to fit. If you want to, paint the planks different colours at this stage. Sand them down once dry to achieve a distressed look.

STEP THREE

Fit the planks into place and attach them with the 1¼in (30mm) wood screws to secure them. Sand the seat well and apply a layer of beeswax to protect the wood (follow the manufacturer's instructions).

STEP FOUR

Fit a flat bit into your drill. Turn the seat part onto its side and drill four holes in each corner of the frame. These will be where the rope goes through to suspend the swing. Ensure the holes are big enough to accommodate your choice of rope.

STEP FIVE

If you want, you can now paint the side supports and sand the back to create a distressed look.

STEP SIX

Now cut three equal lengths of pallet planks to support the back of the swing. For this project, the supports were cut to 15¾in (40cm) in length.

STEP SEVEN

Attach all three supports to the rear of the swing seat with the 1½in (40mm) wood screws. Make sure they are equally spaced out, with one at each end and one in the middle. Once again, you can paint the supports and sand them down.

STEP EIGHT

Now cut two more planks to the exact length of the swing. These will form the back support. Attach them to the supports with the 1¼in (30mm) wood screws. Leave a gap between the seat and the first plank so that when you attach the rope it can fit between.

STEP NINE

Take two more planks and cut them to your desired length for the arms of the swing. Here, the arms were cut a little shorter than the width of the swing. Using your jigsaw, round off one end of each arm. If need be, cut out a small section at the other end so that the arm butts up to the back support and fits over the plank acting as the back support. Sand the arms well.

STEP TEN

To attach the arms, using the 1½in (40mm) screws, drill the screws into the back support arms straight through into the ends of the arms.

STEP ELEVEN

Turn the seat on its side and put another two screws up into the bottom of each arm. This will pull the back tight to the arms and keep it upright and strong to withstand the swinging action.

STEP TWELVE

Measure the height of the branch or support from which you are going to hang the swing so you can determine the length of rope needed. Once you have done this, cut the rope in half using heavy-duty scissors – you will need a length of rope for each side of the swing. Taking one end of the rope, put it through the hole in the front and pass it all the way through to the hole at the back, pulling it through and up under the bottom of the first support plank at the back. Tie a knot in the other end, leaving a single piece of rope attached at the knot that will then go over your branch or support to hang the tree. Repeat this process on the other side, making sure that the height of the knot is the same on both sides.

STEP THIRTEEN

With the help of a friend, hang your swing up securely. Make sure before you hang your tree that the branch you are attaching it to can take the weight of the swing with the added weight of one or two people. Test this thoroughly by hanging off the branch and bouncing until you are happy it is safe! Throw a blanket over the seat for comfort, and swing away.

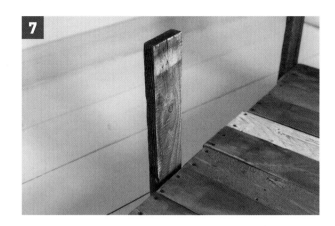

COFFEE TABLE

Turn a simple pallet into a super-cool coffee table for your living area. The diagonal slats add a striking design element. You could add extra detail by painting each slat a different colour, or keep it simple with a wax finish. Either way, this piece is a show-stopper.

YOU WILL NEED

1 x American pallet (chosen for its shaped detailing),
   plus several extra pallet planks

Handsaw or jigsaw

Pencil or marker pen

Ruler or tape measure

Drill

1¼in (30mm) wood screws

Wood glue

Sander and sandpaper (120-grit)

Oak wood stain and cloth to apply it (optional)

Beeswax and cloth to apply it (optional)

Wood filler (optional)

4 x metal hairpin legs (these are usually sold with screws
   included, otherwise you will also need to purchase
   the correct size and number of screws for the legs)

STEP ONE

Take a pallet and cut it down the middle lengthways. Cut to one side of the middle support: you will need that support attached to the half from which you make the tabletop, as it will form one of the sides.

STEP TWO

Cut four planks to fit as a frame on top of the half of the pallet you are using and put them to one side.

STEP THREE

Take several extra planks and lay them on a flat surface. Place the pieces of the frame onto the planks so that it is square with the planks beneath at an angle to get a diagonal pattern showing through underneath.

STEP FOUR

Once you are happy with the position of your frame and planks, take a pencil or marker pen and mark a line on the inside of the frame onto the planks. Now you have your cut marks.

STEP FIVE

Take each plank and cut along the lines on each one with a jigsaw or handsaw. To make sure you don't confuse each piece and remember the sequence in which they go, you can write a number on the back to remind you.

STEP SIX

Put the pieces you have cut together: they should form a perfect rectangle.

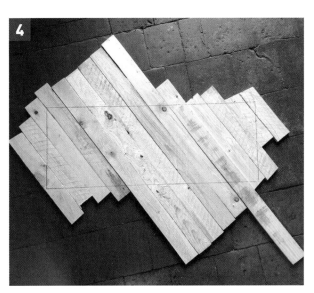

STEP SEVEN

Place the frame on top of the half pallet you cut earlier and secure them with either wood glue or 1¼in (30mm) wood screws. Cover the exposed slats with wood glue and start to put the pieces of plank into the middle of the frame to create the central pattern inside the frame of the tabletop.

STEP EIGHT

Continue until you have completed the build of the tabletop.

STEP NINE

Now create the decorative look you want. Sand the pallet and planks so that they are smooth, rounding off any corners. You could paint the planks if you like, but here I used an oak wood stain applied with a cloth. If there are any gaps where your cuts were a little short on your internal section, use wood filler to fill them. Lightly sand once more when the stain has dried. Then, using another cloth, apply some natural beeswax to give the table a smooth finish. The tabletop is now complete.

STEP TEN

For the legs, you will need four metal hairpin legs 10–12in (25–30cm) in height. These simply screw to the bottom of the pallet.

STEP ELEVEN

Turn the table over, stand it on its legs and voilà!

TOWEL RAIL SHELVES

Space is always at a premium in the bathroom. These shelves not only look great in both modern and traditional bathrooms, but are useful too, providing a hanging rail for towels and storage for toiletries and bathroom essentials.

YOU WILL NEED

1 x standard-sized pallet (an American pallet was
   used here for its shaped detailing)
Tools to remove planks (see page 14)
Jigsaw
Sander and sandpaper (120-grit)
Drill
1¼in (30mm) wood screws
⅝in (15mm) flat wood drill bit
⅝in (15mm) copper plumbing pipe
Pipe cutter
Epoxy glue
2 x ⅝in (15mm) end caps for the copper pipe

STEP ONE

Take a pallet and place it upside down on the ground. Decide which end you are going to use, then remove the planks (see page 13) from the end of that half. Now cut the pallet in half.

STEP TWO

The three supports should be protruding slightly. Round off these ends with the jigsaw and sand them until they are smooth.

STEP THREE

Sand the whole section you are using very thoroughly. Make sure to sand the corners and edges, rounding and smoothing them off where necessary.

STEP FOUR

Now you need a few lengths of pallet wood to fill in the two gaps in the back of your unit. Cut the lengths to fit and attach them to the three supports from behind with 1$\frac{1}{4}$in (30mm) wood screws.

STEP FIVE

For the top of the shelf, use a slightly wider pallet plank. Cut it so that it is slightly longer than the shelf's width; when attached, it should stick out 1$\frac{1}{4}$ or 1$\frac{1}{2}$in (30–40mm) each side. Attach the plank with 1$\frac{1}{4}$in (30mm) wood screws.

STEP SIX

Using the planks that you removed at the beginning, measure the two spaces between the middle and end supports and cut two lengths of plank to fit between the supports. These will form the base of the shelf.

STEP SEVEN

Turn the whole piece over and attach the shelf bottoms with 1$\frac{1}{4}$in (30mm) wood screws from the back.

STEP EIGHT

Now attach a wider plank to the front at the bottom to make the front of the shelf. Attach with 1$\frac{1}{4}$in (30mm) wood screws.

STEP NINE

Taking your $\frac{5}{8}$in (15mm) flat wood drill bit, make a hole in the middle of each of the bottom of the three supports to enable you to push the $\frac{5}{8}$in (15mm) copper pipe through to create the towel rail.

STEP TEN

Push the copper pipe through. Cut off any excess pipe with a pipe cutter. Put a few dabs of epoxy glue onto the ends of the pipe and place on the end caps.

FOOTSTOOL

This little footstool is both practical and comfortable and adds an appealing feature to a living room. You can keep the planks natural, use a wood stain to enhance the grain or paint it to co-ordinate with other elements in the room. Finally, pick out a hard-wearing fabric for the seat cover.

YOU WILL NEED

Planks from 2 pallets (any type)
Tools for removing planks (see page 14)
11ft 6in (3.5m) length of 2 x 4in wooden batten
Handsaw
Jigsaw
Sander and sandpaper (120-grit)
Drill
1¼in (30mm) and 1½in (40mm) wood screws
Piece of foam (suggested thickness: 4in/10cm)
Marker pen
Fabric for seat cover (approx. 31½ x 31½in/80 x 80cm)
Scissors
Staple gun and staples
Beeswax and clean cloth to apply it

STEP ONE

Cut four pieces of 2 x 4in (5–10cm) battens to approximately 15¾in (40cm) in length. These will form the corner supports of the stool to which the four sides will be attached later.

STEP TWO

Next, decide how big you want the footstool to be. The one shown here was 19¾ x 19¾in (50 x 50cm). To achieve this, cut six pallet planks to 19¾in (50cm) in length.

STEP THREE

Cut another six pallet planks to 17¾in (45cm). These will clad the four sides of the footstool. You will use three planks for each side to make a frame height of 12in (30cm), assuming the width of pallet plank is about 4in (10cm). Sand all your planks down before attaching them to ensure there are no spiky corners.

STEP FOUR

Two of the sides plank are cut to 17¾in (45cm) as these will sit into the other planks, bringing the full width to 19¾in (50cm): this takes into consideration the width of the planks of the two other sides it will sit in against once you attach it all together.

STEP FIVE

Take two battens and start to attach the 19¾in (50cm) planks to them to create the first side using 1½in (40mm) wood screws. Leave a 1in (25mm) space between the top planks and the end of the batten and the same to the left and right of the battens. Repeat this process so you have two sides of the footstool prepared.

STEP SIX

Now take the shorter planks and attach them to the sides of the battens using 1½in (40mm) wood screws (this is why you left a 1in/25mm space). This will give you the 19¾ x 19¾in (50 x 50cm) footstool frame once everything is attached.

STEP SEVEN

The seat part of the stool needs to be supported from within. Next, cut two more pieces of batten so that they fit between two sides of the corner supports and attach with 1½in (40mm) wood screws.

STEP EIGHT

If the feet stick out at the bottom, using a handsaw, cut them off square with the bottom of the last plank.

STEP NINE

To make the top of the seat, cut more planks to fit across the inner frame.

STEP TEN

Place your hand over the planks and turn the frame upside down so that the seat is on the floor. Now attach two planks to secure the seat planks together using 1¼in (30mm) wood screws. This will create a removable seat.

STEP ELEVEN

Take the foam and place the seat on top of it. Draw around it with a marker pen so that you can cut the foam to size.

STEP TWELVE

Now take the covering fabric. Make sure that it is at least 4in (10cm) bigger than your seat all the way around. Place the foam on top of the material in the centre. Then place the seat onto the foam and fold the material up and around the foam. Attach it with a staple gun to the bottom part of the seat.

STEP THIRTEEN

Once you have attached all of the material, fold in the corners so that they are neat. Turn the seat over and place it into the frame of the footstool, pushing it firmly so that it sits down onto the inner frame. Use beeswax on the frame to give the stool a more finished look.

TIP

Foam comes in different thicknesses and levels of firmness. Here, foam with a 4in (10cm) thickness and medium level of firmness was used. Medium firmness is recommended over hard, as it wants to have some give in it.

WINE RACK

Combining practical storage with homemade chic, this rack will look great hanging on the wall in your kitchen or in the garden next to the barbecue area, ready for your guests to help themselves to a glass or two.

YOU WILL NEED

1 x standard-sized pallet (if it's to be used outside then it's best if it's hardwood; an American pallet was used here for its shaped detailing and durability outside)

Handsaw

Jigsaw

Tools to remove planks (see page 14)

Sander and sandpaper (120-grit)

Drill

1¼in (30mm) wood screws

Pencil or marker pen

Enamel house number plaque (optional)

STEP ONE

Take a pallet and cut it in half. Choose the better half of the pallet, turn it over to expose the rear of the pallet and remove the top plank (see page 13).

STEP TWO

Sand down the pallet and smooth off any rough edges and corners.

STEP THREE

Take the plank you removed earlier. Secure it to the bottom of the wine rack using two 1¼in (30mm) wood screws at either end and two in the middle. This will be where your bottles will sit so you want it to be secure.

STEP FOUR

Take a wide plank and cut it slightly longer than the width of the pallet. This plank will be secured to the top of the rack and will be where your glasses will hang. Use a jigsaw to cut six notches into the top plank. Draw the shape onto the wood first so that you can follow the line with your jigsaw, making it easier to obtain a uniform shape.

STEP FIVE

Secure the top to the wine rack with wood screws. I chose to decorate this item with an enamel house number plaque; use your imagination to personalize your wine rack.

TIPI

This handmade tipi will make a wonderful place for children to play in, or a unique addition to your garden. It is an easy project to make and there are many ways you can decorate it to personalize it: wrap bunting around it; cover it in fairy lights; or simply throw in a blanket and some cushions.

YOU WILL NEED

Pallet planks (any type, but if it's to be used outside then it's best if they're hardwood; the number required will depend on the size of tipi you want to make)

4 x 1 x 2in (25 x 50mm) wooden battens

Handsaw or jigsaw

Drill

1¼in (30mm) wood screws

Sander and sandpaper (120-grit)

Materials to decorate tipi (chalk paint, for example)

STEP ONE

First, decide how big you want the tipi to be. The length of the battens will determine the height of the tipi. In this project, the four battens that create the tipi framework were cut to 59in (150cm) in length. Cut your four battens for the frame to equal length and set two of the battens aside.

Take two battens and lay them flat on the ground so that you can establish the internal size of your tipi. The wider the battens go out at the bottom, the larger the floor space and the lower your tipi will be. Sand the planks before you attach them; this will not only save time, but ensure that they are as safe and smooth as possible if children are using the tipi.

Once you are happy with the angle, take a plank and place one at the bottom of the two battens widest apart. Secure them in place with a 1¼in (30mm) wood screw into each batten. This will secure the battens, and the correct angle desired, in place so that you can start to add planks to create the first side of your tipi.

STEP TWO

Repeat this process all the way up the battens to the top. You can space your planks as close or far apart as you like. Here, they were spaced with about 4in (10cm) between them.

STEP THREE

Turn the frame you have created over onto a flat surface and cut off the excess plank.

STEP FOUR

You should be left with a neat triangular frame that will form one of the sides of the tipi.

STEP FIVE

Now you need to repeat this process. The easiest way to make sure your two triangular frames are identical in size is to lay down the other two battens you cut earlier on top of the battens attached to the planks.

STEP SIX

Once these are perfectly lined up, lay down your planks again and secure them with 1¼in (30mm) wood screws. Once again, turn the frame upside down flat on the ground and cut off the excess planks to create the second, identical triangular frame.

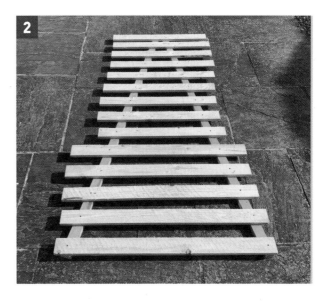

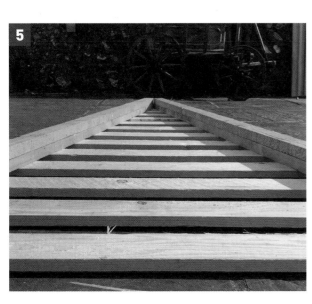

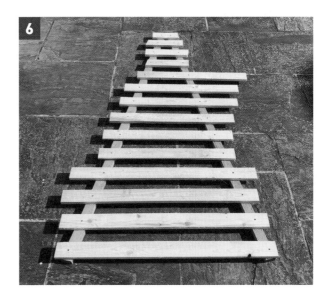

STEP SEVEN

Stand the two sides up and lean them up against one another to make sure that the space between the frames is the same width as the width of the bottom of the frame. This will ensure the tipi has a nice square floor space. Attach the two sides together at the top using a short pice of plank, which you need to screw into both of the frames.

STEP EIGHT

Now attach more planks all the way down the back of the tipi, again cutting off the excess planks to form clean corners. The tipi should be taking shape now, as all three sides will be attached to it.

STEP NINE

Now work on the front. You will need an entrance to your tipi. Cut two planks to approximately 39in (100cm) each in length, then cut the tops of them at a slight angle. These can be attached to the front sides of the tipi to create a doorframe going upwards vertically. If you cut them at an angle, this creates a straight line to which the planks can be attached above them. This also makes the front look neater as it covers the ends of the planks used to create the sides.

STEP TEN

Attach more planks above the legs to create the top of the entrance. Cut the planks to the correct length to finish them off, as you did before.

STEP ELEVEN

To finish off the entrance, screw one more plank to the bottom front plank so that it protrudes slightly, and cut the excess plank off as before. You can use this area to decorate with a child's name, or paint a picture over the entrance.

STEP TWELVE

Decorate the tipi however you like. I painted the tipi white and added a flag to the top.

TIP

Why not train plants over the tipi to turn it into a secret, hidden den?

DARTBOARD HOUSING

The problem with hanging a dartboard on a wall is that you often end up with more holes in the wall than you do in the board! This pallet dartboard housing solves that dilemma and looks great too. Depending on the style of your home, you might like to choose a different finish: why not try a smart dark wood stain, or paint each slat a different colour?

YOU WILL NEED

Pallet planks (any type; the number required will depend on the size of dartboard housing you want to make)

Handsaw or jigsaw

Drill

1¼in (30mm) and 1½in (40mm) wood screws

Wood drill bit

Pencil

2 x picture loops and nails/hooks to hang up the housing

STEP ONE

First, measure the space where you will be hanging this project. Once you have established the space you have available, you can calculate the size of your project. I worked to a height of 47in (120cm) and a width of 31½in (80cm) to ensure that there was enough room for the shelf and the board without it being too cramped. Cut the two sides and the top and bottom of the planks and attach them with 1¼in (30mm) wood screws to create the frame.

STEP TWO

Next, cut enough planks to the exact length of the frame to cover the entire back of the frame. Once you have cut them to size, lay them down next to each other. Push them up snugly against each other with no gaps.

STEP THREE

Once you are happy with the position of the planks (ensuring the side you want to see is facing down and away from you), start fixing them to the frame with 1¼in (30mm) wood screws.

STEP FOUR

Once all of the planks are securely attached to the frame, turn the housing over and cut one more plank that will serve as the shelf on which the darts will sit. Attach the shelf to the two sides of the frame using 1½in (40mm) wood screws.

STEP FIVE

With a pencil, make six equally spaced marks on the shelf. Using a wood drill bit, drill small holes where the marks are, large enough for a dart to fit but not so snug that it is hard to pull it out). These will act as the dart holders.

STEP SIX

Hold up your dartboard and decide exactly where you want it to sit in the housing. Put a screw into the back to hang the board on. There are a number of different ways to hang up the dartboard housing. I used two picture loops attached to the rear that will go over hooks or nails on the wall.

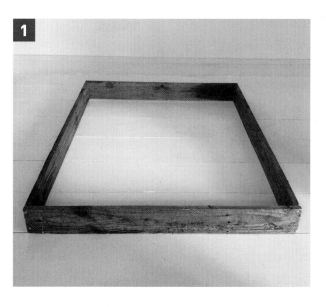

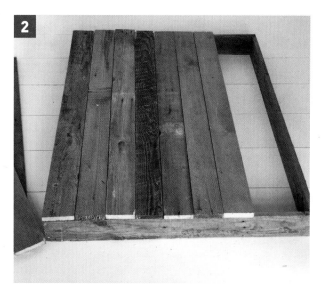

SIDE TABLE

This compact little side table is simple to make and will perfectly fill a gap in any room. Tuck it between two armchairs with an elegant coffee-table book and a candle to add a touch of comfort to your living space.

YOU WILL NEED

Pallet planks (any type; the number required will depend on the size of table you want to make)

1 x 2in (25–50mm) wood battens for frame

Handsaw or jigsaw

Drill

1½in (40mm) and 1¼in (30mm) wood screws

Sander and sandpaper (120-grit)

Danish natural oil and cloth to apply it (optional)

STEP ONE

First decide on the dimensions of your side table, then cut the pallet planks for the base to length. Here, I cut the planks to 19¾in (50cm) in length to create the height of the base. I used five planks on all four sides to create a rough square base.

STEP TWO

Place the five planks (or fewer if you choose to make a smaller table) next to each other on a flat surface. Take the battens and cut them to length to make a frame for the planks, then screw them securely in place with 1½in (40mm) wood screws. Repeat this process for another five planks (or however many you are using).

STEP THREE

Turn the two frames over to reveal the planks. Ensure they are securely attached to the battens, creating strong frames.

STEP FOUR

Find a corner of a room to lean one of the frames up against to ensure it is straight. Position the other frame a short distance from it. Lay extra planks across the top of both frames and attach them to the edges of the battens with 1¼in (30mm) wood screws. This will create the third side of the table base.

STEP FIVE

Once all of the planks are securely attached, turn the piece again and repeat the process for the fourth and final side of the base.

STEP SIX

For the top of the table, cut more planks, but this time slightly wider than the base, to create an overhanging top. Lay them on top of the box, using 1½in (40mm) wood screws to attach each one. Push a little harder than you might think necessary to sink the screws in slightly and ensure they are hidden. To complete the look of your side table, take your sander and sand the sides and top of the table, rounding off the corners and removing any rough edges.

TIP

For a more finished effect, apply natural Danish oil with a cloth to seal the wood.

HEADBOARD

With its striking off-centre diagonal design feature, this bedhead will make a fantastic centrepiece for your bedroom. This project is for a single bed, but you can easily scale it up for a double, queen or king-size bed – the process is exactly the same, no matter what size you are working to.

YOU WILL NEED

Pallet planks (any type; the number required will depend on the dimensions of headboard you want to make)

MDF or chipboard, just larger than the headboard will be

Handsaw, jigsaw or power saw

Drill

1¼in (30mm) wood screws

Tape measure or ruler

Combination square (to set a 45-degree angle)

Pencil or marker pen

Wood glue

Wood filler

Sander and sandpaper (120-grade)

Chalk paint and paintbrush

Beeswax and clean cloth to apply it

STEP ONE

Cut a piece of wood (MDF or chipboard) to just over the width of the bed you are making the headboard for, and establish how high you want it to be from the mattress when it is on the bed. For this project, the dimensions of the headboard were 39in (100cm) wide x 30in (77cm) high. This headboard will be attached to the wall so it does not need legs. To make your frame, take four lengths of wood and cut two of them to the width of the piece of wood and two to the length. Now take each piece of wood and cut the ends at 45-degree angles at both ends. There are several ways to do this: use a power saw that has a 45-degree cutting setting; set a combination square to 45 degrees, or use the 45-degree guide that is on every handsaw.

STEP TWO

Next you will start to cut the planks (note that some of the planks have been painted and sanded to give texture to the design) again using 45-degree angles at both ends. First, you need to cut a perfect triangle. Take the first plank. From the top of the end, draw a 45-degree angle using the 45-degree angle on your handsaw (or use a power saw and combination square as described above) and make your cut.

STEP THREE

For the second plank and all remaining ones, you need to measure the length of the last plank you laid (at its longest side). Mark this length on the middle of a plank, then mark your two 45-degree angles, starting at the marks you made when marking the length on the plank, and draw your cut line outwards.

STEP FOUR

Continue to cut and place the planks down. You will see they all fit neatly together.

STEP FIVE

To create an interesting pattern, draw a line down the middle or one-third of the way across the board, and cut the planks up to the edge of the line. This will allow you to start again on the other side of the line; if your planks are all the same width they should line up neatly.

STEP SIX

Once you are happy with the design of your headboard, remove all of the cut planks and put them aside. Take some wood glue and spread it generously across the board. Lay your planks back down in the correct order and press them into the glue so that they are secure and leave to dry.

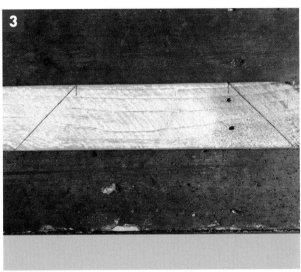

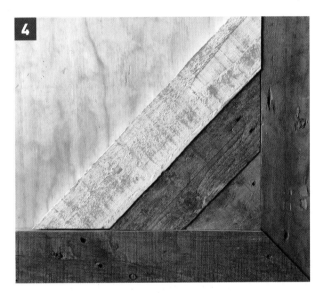

STEP SEVEN

Once the glue has set and your planks are securely in place, take some wood filler and fill the gaps between the planks. With pallet wood, there will always be irregular shapes; the filler helps to even these out a little. Sand all the planks lightly to make sure they are smooth and that the filler isn't visible anywhere other than in the cracks.

STEP EIGHT

Consider the colours of the planks and shapes that they make. For example, here the brown-stained planks all meet up in the middle to create chevrons. If you want to make any changes to the colours or to stain some of the planks, now is the time. Once you are happy with the way your headboard looks, apply some beeswax to the boards using a clean cloth.

STEP NINE

To finish the headboard, cut a plank 4in (10cm) wider than the board and attach it to the top of the headboard with $1\frac{1}{4}$in (30mm) wood screws. The plank should stick out either side by about 2in (50mm). You can attach heavy-duty picture hooks to the back of the frame, then hang it onto screws drilled into the wall. Make sure you use the correct rawl plugs so it's secure and safe (brick walls need plastic rawl plugs; plasterboard walls need metal plasterboard rawl plugs).

GARDEN BENCH

This sturdy bench will add some homespun vibes and sophistication to any area, indoors or out. You could make two, with a fire pit between them, throw on some comfortable cushions and a couple of blankets and chill out under the stars on a summer's evening.

YOU WILL NEED

1 x standard-size pallet (an American pallet was used here for its shaped detailing and durability outside)
International pallet planks
Tools to remove planks (see page 14)
Handsaw or jigsaw
Sander and sandpaper (120-grade)
Drill
1½in (40mm) and 1¼in (30mm) wood screws

STEP ONE

Place the pallet on a flat surface and cut it in half lengthways. Ensure that the side you want to use for the seat part has the middle support attached to it.

STEP TWO

Take the other section of the pallet and remove all of the top planks (see page 13). You will use these to strengthen the seat. Once you have removed them, check that they fit into the spaces between the planks on the seat part of the bench. Here, one needed cutting lengthways to fit into one of the gaps as it was thinner than the others. Generally, they should all fit nicely.

STEP THREE

Because you cut the initial pallet in half keeping one side (the seat side) attached to the middle support, the other half, from which you have just removed the planks, will be slightly shorter, meaning that your planks will be shorter too. This is not a problem: when you place them into the spaces on the seat they will still reach the supports so that you can attach them securely with screws.

STEP FOUR

Now attach the legs. For these you will need the wider parts that attach the ends of a pallet. Remove four of these from a separate pallet, or use pallet planks that you have already bought in lengths and cut them to size. The important thing is that they are the wide planks and are solid. The legs for this project were cut to 23½in (60cm) in length. Once you have them cut and sanded, attach them to each corner of the pallet seat using 1½in (40mm) wood screws.

STEP FIVE

Now make the arms of the bench. Cut two parts of pallet plank to 23½in (60cm) in length. Sand them well, rounding off the corners of one end of each plank for a neat finish. Attach these to the legs with 1¼in (30mm) wood screws, making sure that the back of the arm is flush with the end of the rear leg and the front is protruding.

STEP SIX

You should now have your seat with legs and arms attached.

TIP

Choosing pallets with nice, natural colouring means you can leave the planks bare. If, however, you're not keen on the colour, then you can always stain or paint the planks.

STEP SEVEN

The final part of the project is to make the back of the bench. Cut two lengths of international (longer-length) pallet planks to fit between the legs. Secure the two planks, which will serve as the back of your bench, to the legs and arms.

STEP EIGHT

Cut two more pieces of plank to about 20¾in (53cm) (or whatever the distance is edge to edge of the rear and front leg) and attach the leg supports. These will give strength to the bench.

STEP NINE

Your bench is now complete. You can dress it however you desire. Here I used a French grain sack with feather stuffing for the rear cushion, and an oversized cushion for the seat. Both make attractive additions to the bench and make it usable for both indoor and outdoor purposes.

BATH RACK

*This project adds a modern twist to the old-fashioned bath tray.
Combining convenience and style, it will allow you to enjoy a bath
with a glass of wine and a book within easy reach.*

YOU WILL NEED

Pallet planks (any type; the number required will depend
    on the size of tray you want to make)
Jigsaw
Sander and sandpaper (120-grade)
Pencil or marker pen
Ruler
Drill
1½in (40mm) and 1¼in (30mm) wood screws
Tile glue
1 tile, 8 x 4in (20 x 10cm)
Wood glue
A small cup

STEP ONE

First measure the width of the bath for which you are making the tray, as baths vary in size. This tray had internal width measurements of 25½in (65cm). Cut two lengths of plank to 24in (61cm) each. These will form the bottom of the tray. Sand down each plank that you cut so that it is smooth. This will give your project a more finished look and will also ensure you don't get splinters.

STEP TWO

Cut another plank to 32in (81cm), then cut the plank lengthways down the middle so that you have two equal pieces. These will form the sides of the tray.

STEP THREE

Next cut another plank to 8in (20cm) in length, then cut the plank in half lengthways. These will form the ends of your tray.

STEP FOUR

Take the two pieces for the sides and draw a 3⅛ x ¾in (8 x 2cm) box at each bottom corner.

STEP FIVE

Take a small cup and place it as shown to draw a perfect curve between the two lines.

STEP SIX

Repeat this process on the other side of the plank. Use your jigsaw to cut out the shape you have drawn. You are creating the dips that will enable the tray to sit safely over the curve of the side of the bath. Sand the curves to ensure they are smooth, with no rough edges.

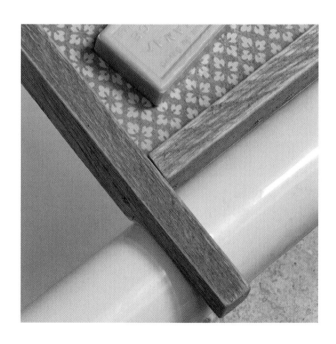

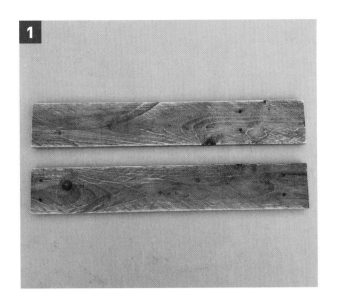

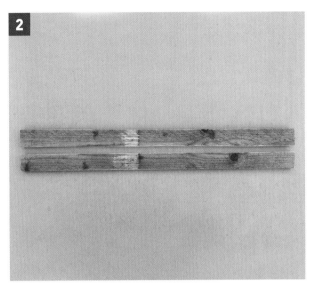

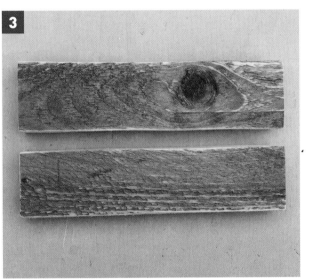

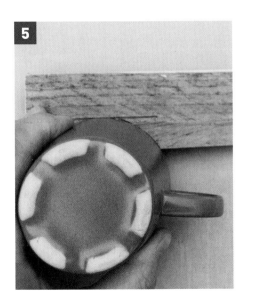

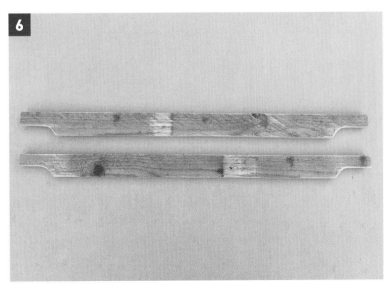

STEP SEVEN

Take the two planks that were cut to form the bottom of the tray in step one and attach the two end pieces you cut in step three. Use two 1½in (40mm) wood screws in each plank to ensure it is fixed properly.

STEP EIGHT

Use 1¼in (30mm) wood screws to attach the sides to the ends of the tray.

STEP NINE

Next you will make the soapdish using a tile. Most tile stores sell tiles that measure 8 x 4in (20 x 10cm), which is what I used here. Put a little tile glue on the bottom and stick it down to the tray. Cut one more plank in half so that it measures 1in (25mm) high (the tray's internal height measurement) and 8in (20cm) in length. Attach this to the other side of the tile with wood glue to finish off the soapdish.

STEP TEN

To finish off the bath tray, cut one more plank lengthways ¾in (20mm) in width and 8in (200mm) in length and apply wood glue to the rear. Place this in the middle of the tray ⅝in (15mm) away from the side. This will serve as a bookstand.

RESOURCES

UK

Pallets

Check local suppliers' listings for wood stores in your area.

All Pallets

www.allpallets.co.uk

For international (longer-length) pallets:

The Pallet Company

www.thepalletcompany.co.uk

The Wood Store

www.woodrecycling.org.uk

For DIY supplies (tools, screws, paint, etc.)

B&Q

www.diy.com

Homebase

www.homebase.co.uk

Screw Fix

www.screwfix.com

Travis Perkins

www.travisperkins.co.uk

USA

Pallets

Check local suppliers' listings for wood stores in your area.

All Size Pallets

www.allsizepallets.com

Pallet One

www.palletone.com

For DIY supplies (tools, screws, paint, etc.)

Ace Hardware

www.acehardware.com

Home Depot

www.homedepot.com

Lowes

www.lowes.com

Menards

www.menards.com

INDEX

To order a book, or to request a catalogue, contact:

GMC Publications Ltd

Castle Place, 166 High Street,

Lewes, East Sussex,

BN7 1XU

United Kingdom

Tel: +44 (0)1273 488005

www.gmcbooks.com